The ten major types of Black racism include illegal employment discrimination against Whites, Black-on-White crime and various types of casual racism that target Whites for harassment. Although Whites experience these forms of Black racism at work, in school and on the street, many Blacks pretend that Black racism does not exist, and do so for reasons they are careful to conceal from Whites. Both Black racism and the blanket denials that it exists are actually reflections of a covert mindset that legitimizes crimes and other forms of victimization of Whites. Most Whites know little about why this mindset developed, why it persists and who benefits from the conspiracy of silence that denies the existence and practice of Black-on-White racism.

Black Racism, White Victims

Reverse Discrimination, Black-On-White Crime And Other Legal Problems

JOHN PUBLIUS

Black Racism, White Victims

Reverse Discrimination, Black-On-White Crime And Other Legal Problems

Copyright © 2011 by John Publius (pseudonym)
All rights reserved.

https://www.Createspace.com/3631825

ISBN-10: 1463598386
ISBN-13: 9781463598389

Table Of Contents

1   Chapter One
       Discrimination Against Whites

11   Chapter Two
       The Ten Types Of Black Racism

33   Chapter Three
       Blacks Who Identify With The Aggressor

41   Chapter Four
       The Secret History Of Black Racism

55   Chapter Five
       Blacks Who Pretend That
       Black Racism Does Not Exist

67   Chapter Six
       Ghetto Racism And Crime

81   Chapter Seven
       The Psychology Of Black Racism

91   Chapter Eight
       Other Forms Of Black Racism

99   Chapter Nine
       Legal Options

115   Chapter Ten
       Black-On-White Crime Statistics

119   Court Cases And Other References

Chapter One: Discrimination Against Whites

Chapter One: Discrimination Against Whites

Legal Background

Several U.S. Supreme Court cases have found reverse discrimination against Whites to be illegal, but reverse discrimination continues to be perpetrated against Whites. Who is doing this, why do they do it?

Black-on-White crime is several times larger in magnitude than the opposite situation, despite Blacks constituting only one-eighth of the total U.S. population. Why does this crime trend exist?

The Supreme Court has ruled that preferring members of any one group for no reason other than race or ethnic origin constitutes illegal discrimination. Thus, any sort of behavior that would be considered racist when perpetrated by a White against a Black, is automatically regarded as being racist when such behavior perpetrated by a Black against a White.

The best explanation is the explanation that most readily fits all of the facts. If something looks like a duck, walks like a duck and quacks like a duck, it is a duck, period. Evidence is everything and excuses are nothing. Those who uphold two different sets of standards for Whites and Blacks, meaning double standards, is a racist.

Black racism consists of crimes and discrimination perpetrated by Blacks against Whites, as well as Asians, foreign-born Blacks and Blacks who act "White." Blacks who discriminate against Whites and commit crimes against Whites are racists. Black-on-White discrimination is racism. Black-on-White crime is racism. Double standards for Blacks and Whites constitutes racism.

When a Black racist claims to not be a racist because he is of the opinion that Blacks are incapable of being racists, he is lying. It is up to such Black racists to prove the correctness of their opinions when the facts spell out they are lying. Whites do not need permission from Blacks to think of, and label, Blacks as racists, any more than the victims of a thief need the permission of the thief to classify him as being a thief and prosecute him for theft. Those who are under scrutiny by their victims cannot be allowed to decide what can and cannot be included in their victims' definition of racism.

Black racism exists regardless of how many Blacks deny that it exists. Denials of the existence of Black racism in the face of Black-on-White crime statistics and reverse discrimination court cases are pathetically laughable. The evidence exists regardless of the willful pretenses put forth by those who claim that such evidence does not exist or does not fit their personal definitions of racism. People who are under scrutiny always say such things and always attempt to stop others from reaching the conclusions that the facts point towards. They have a lot to hide and work at hiding it.

Many Black racists say that accusing them of racism is racism, but lies of that sort are suitable only for derision. Evidence in the form of crime statistics, anti-White employment discrimination and college admission discrimination add up to the conclusion that Black racism is very much alive and well. Ask their victims. Knowing the truth allows you to make the truth as you know it into the basis for your daily thoughts, decisions and actions.

When Whites charge Black racists with being racists, those whites typically find themselves automatically accused of being racists. Lies are standard operating procedure for Black racists, most of whom are criminals who have made careers out of denying their criminal behavior. Lies promulgated by Black racists are intended to mislead Whites and mislead Whites towards ends that serve the self-interest of Black racists. If you disbelieve Black racists, you will have many fewer problems in life. Use your best judgment in passing judgment on black racists and take action on it.

Black racists routinely promulgate a Big Lie to the effect that Blacks do not discriminate or engage in racism because they claim that Blacks are incapable of being racists for an unspecified reason that they refuse to disclose to Whites. No verifiable proof has ever been offered to back up such claims, so their denials prove nothing until such time as verifiable proof is forthcoming and delivered. Denials of the existence of Black racism on the part of Black racists are contradicted by mountains of evidence in the form of Black-on-White crime statistics and court decisions that have struck down reverse discrimination perpetuated by Blacks against Whites.

Blacks routinely characterize themselves as being members of a group that has experienced racial discrimination. However, quite a few Blacks have shown themselves to be fully capable of perpetrating racism themselves, fully capable of lying about the racism they perpetrate, fully capable of covering up and misrepresenting their lies and fully capable of denying their racism because they choose to lie about it. Criminals often do such things. The best starting point for inquiry is the victims of Black racists, not the perpetrators.

Black racists perpetrate discrimination and racist criminal violence against Whites, Asians and foreign-born Blacks. Black-on-Black discrimination is so common that there are both civil court cases and movies about social discrimination perpetrated by light-skinned Blacks against dark-skinned Blacks. Both civil and criminal courts offer numerous records of contemporary Black-on-White crimes.

During the era of slavery, some freed Blacks kept other Blacks as their slaves, and some Blacks worked as whip-wielding plantation overseers, unpalatable but easily-verifiable historical truths that contemporary Blacks do not want to be bothered with. The theory that Blacks are incapable of discrimination or racism is thus an outright lie contradicted at every turn by contemporary criminal court records, civil court decisions and historical records. The ugly facts always show that the ugly Black racists are lying.

Truth And Falsehood

Someone once said that if you tell a big enough lie frequently enough, people will start to believe it because they would not believe that anyone would have the nerve to willfully lie in such a manner. The reality of the matter is that a lie remains a lie no matter how big it is, no matter how often it is trotted out as being the supposed truth, regardless of who trots out that lie and no matter what the details of that lie are.

If someone tells you that two plus two equals three, that statement is a lie no matter how often that lie is repeated or who repeats it. Black racists lie to Whites because they have a secret agenda. Blacks who have obtained college admission or employment through reverse discrimination are unlikely and unwilling to admit that anything that has benefited them personally could possibly be bad, though their victims see things quite differently than the beneficiaries of such illegal activities. Upton Sinclair was correct when he said that it is difficult to get a man to understand something when his job depends on not understanding it, and that includes pretending to not understand something by denying that it exists at all.

Intellectually unsupportable denials of the existence of Black racism are promulgated by Black racists for the purpose of steering Whites' thoughts and actions in directions that promote the personal interests of Black racists. They want Whites to believe that nothing is wrong with employment discrimination that targets Whites and Black on-White crimes that targets Whites.

Black racism exists in every social class. The higher a Black racist's social class, however, the more likely it is that the Black racist has daily contact with Whites in some sort of organization where outright hostility to Whites is cause for termination of employment. Blacks racists employed in white-collar settings are usually quite careful to disguise their anti-White sentiments and behavior in order to avoid unpleasant outcomes. Their activities often take the form of fraud or manipulation, such as finding a superficially plausible, but bogus, rationale for discriminating against Whites while using a very different standard with respect to Blacks.

Black racists in blue-collar work environments often operate in groups that are the workplace equivalent of street gangs. They conspire against Whites, and do do so because they enjoy pushing White victims around and enjoy bragging about their activities to other sadistic Black racists. Once you understand that they simply do not like Whites, their activities become much easier to understand.

Black racists who witness attacks on Whites by other Black racists routinely claim to have seen nothing. You'll never see a Black racist help prosecute, or terminate from employment, other Black racists, because they are often members of the same formal or informal gang in the workplace.

Their racism can take on forms such as avoiding punishing Blacks who express ant-White sentiments or even outright violence against Whites. Whites should always distrust Black racists motivated by the impulse to punish whites, meaning the sort of Blacks who go out of their way to put down and victimize Whites because they are White. Black favoritism is anti-White racism, and is a form of discrimination.

Blacks who run their own businesses are capable of perpetrating racism against Whites, and are able to set things up so as to ensure that no witnesses are ever present to witness their personal brand of Black racism in action. Among members of the ghetto social classes, anti-White racism is blatant, public, undisguised, physical and often involves gang-style collaboration, while tending to be disguised and of a nonphysical nature in the white-collar social classes.

The solution to the Big Lie is the Big Truth: ongoing discussion by Whites that some Blacks are racists who hate and envy Whites because they are White. This includes acknowledging that Black racists work at putting their racist beliefs into action on the job, on the street and in schools, knowing that Black racists routinely lie about their own racism and the racism of other Blacks with a straight face, and knowing that Black racists demand that both Blacks and Whites turn a blind eye to their activities because they feel entitled to avoid punishment for anti-White racism.

An irrational belief on the part of Black racists that they are entitled to do whatever they want to Whites does not constitute an obligation on the part of Whites to believe anything they say, acquiesce to their wishes or fail to press criminal charges when the White victims of Black racists consider it to be appropriate.

Chapter Two
The Ten Types Of Black Racism

Chapter Two
The Ten Types Of Black Racism

Black racism is a continuum of different types and degrees of anti-White hostility that can range from mental categorization to spoken words to anti-White employment discrimination to anti-White criminal violence. There are ten major types of Black racism.

The First Type Of Black Racism

The first type of Black racism is the use of double standards for speech, behavior and other activities that favor Blacks and discriminate against, or penalize, Whites when members of both races engage in exactly the same behavior. This applies to the law, everyday behavior, education, the workplace and other social contexts.

The purpose of the double standards applied by Black racists to Whites is to devalue Whites as a group, strip Whites of their human rights and treat Whites as second-class citizens without explicitly admitting, or even denying, that the Black racist perpetrators are doing exactly that. For example, denying admission to White public college applicants while simultaneously admitting Black public college applicants who have lower grades and lower scores on the standardized tests taken by both White and Black applicants is an example of an illegal Black racist double standard in action.

According to the US Supreme Court, discrimination on the basis of race is illegal. "Preferring members of any one group for no reason other than race or ethnic origin is discrimination for its own sake," according to Regents of the University of California v. Allan Bakke, a 1978 US Supreme Court case involving public university admission. This sort of practice is completely illegal but nevertheless happens.

Civil service tests that discriminate against Whites based on their race are in violation of Title VII of the Civil Rights Act of 1964, which prohibits intentional acts of employment discrimination based on race, color, religion, sex, and national origin, according to Ricci, et al. v. DeStefano, et al., a 2009 US Supreme Court case. This sort of practice is completely illegal but nevertheless happens.

A typical example of a double standard occurs where some parties make it permissible for Blacks to engage in certain types of behavior, and no action is taken against Black perpetrators, while engaging in selectively different forms of reaction and punishment when Whites are involved.
For example, punishing Whites in a high school lunchroom for a food fight while ignoring and not

punishing Blacks who engaged in the exact same behavior is Black racism. Racial preferences that favor Blacks while denying Whites the same preferences are illegal but nevertheless happen.

Double-standard Black racism is in evidence when Black criminals attack a White and the Blacks who witness the crime and give a pass to the Black crime perpetrator by allowing that perpetrator to go free. Double-standard Black racism is based on the underlying belief that Whites do not have the same rights as Blacks. This sort of practice is completely illegal but nevertheless happens. Perpetrators of double-standard Black racism often retaliate, or attempt to retaliate against Whites who have the gall to act as if they have the same rights to free speech, fair employment, self-defense, and other rights, as Blacks. This often constitutes criminal behavior. It is illegal to retaliate against Whites who use the law and the courts to enforce their rights. The civil rights of Whites include the unlimited right to speak out against Black-on-White employment discrimination and other forms of Black racism.

This form of Black racism is evidence of a lack of respect for Whites.

The Second Type Of Black Racism

The second type of Black racism is casual Black racism of the sort found among Blacks of every social class who engage in the practice of expressing anti-White racism in their everyday words and actions, either by speaking directly to other Blacks or by forcing Whites to listen to what they say to other Blacks in public settings. This sort of behavior may meet the legal definition of harassment if it occurs in the workplace.

A middle-class suburban Black who says that he hates White because of what "they" did to his ancestors is guilty of casual racism. This sort of speech on his part does not directly impact any Whites but does reflect his lack of respect for Whites as a group because he blames contemporary Whites for what Whites who lived long ago did.

A middle-class suburban Black who says that he hates Whites as a group because they are White, but takes no action against Whites other than saying things that some Whites may find abhorrent, is a casual racist.

Incidentally, none of the Whites who had anything to do with slavery are still alive, and none of the Blacks who were impacted by slavery are still alive. Whites are not responsible for the actions of their own ancestors, other people's ancestors or other adults in general. Individual adult Whites are generally responsible only for their own behavior and not the behavior of others.

A Black who rides a bus to work every day and tells another Black that she hates Whites because they put her cousin or boyfriend into jail for drug dealing is a casual racist who does not directly impact any Whites, though she might upset Whites who do not feel like being forced to listen to her opinions on the bus.

A Black who works in a large company, eats in the cafeteria every day for lunch and tells other Blacks that she never met a White who was not a racist is guilty of casual racism.

This sort of racist speech on the part of Blacks can alert White co-workers who have no choice about working with her that she is a casual Black racist of the sort who probably cannot be counted on to call the police if a White person is attacked by a Black felon on the job. That Black felon may be someone she helped obtain a job on the loading dock by conveniently forgetting to do a criminal records check before putting that Black felon on the payroll.

None of these examples of casual Black racism involve any sort of direct threats or violence or direct expressions of racism to Whites.

This form of Black racism is evidence of a lack of respect for Whites.

The Third Type Of Black Racism

The third type of Black racism takes the form of deliberate verbal discourtesy specifically directed against individual Whites, including specific Whites with whom the Black racist may be previously acquainted, such as a bus driver and the driver's passengers on a regular bus route.

When Black racists eat in restaurants where all of the staff members are White, they might make a point of leaving no tip, dropping as much garbage as possible on the floor and laughing about what they have done at the top of their lungs as they exit the restaurant. This is Black racist discourtesy.

When such Black racists use a public library, they talk at the top of their lungs, unlike White patrons, throw things around, and bring drinks and food into parts of the library where such things are not allowed. This is Black racist discourtesy.

Talking at the top of one's lungs in public on a cell phone for the purpose of upsetting Whites is another example. This is Black racist discourtesy.

The public speech of Black racists is often heavily laced with references to sexual activities, and they make a point of ensuring that their volume is loud enough for Whites to hear what they say. They do this because they feel important when they get in the way of Whites or make Whites feel uncomfortable. Neurotics who lead meaningless lives often do such things. This is Black racist discourtesy.

These types of behavior are usually not illegal, but are considered to be perfectly normal behavior in the ghettos from which many Black racists come. You can take the racists out of the ghetto, but can't take the ghetto out of the racists, especially when they come into contact with Whites.

This form of Black racism is evidence of a lack of respect for Whites.

The Fourth Type Of Black Racism

The fourth type of Black racism is the on-the-job practice of illegal discrimination against Whites in employment-related matters and college admissions.

Blacks like to say that racism equals prejudice plus power. Their whole-hearted support for this notion ends when Whites decide to apply this belief to Blacks in general and Black racists in particular. This is another example of a double standard applied by Blacks to Whites. Saying that this notion applies only to Whites and not to Blacks is an automatic warning sign that they are lying through their teeth.

Human resources departments in corporations are good hunting grounds for Blacks who want to discriminate against Whites in the context of employment. Employment discrimination usually occurs during the employment application, hiring, and promotion processes. There are rarely any White witnesses to such activities, but if all of the parties involved in discrimination are Black, you can be sure that some sort of preferential hiring is going on. Blame the Black racists who were present when the discrimination was put into effect.

If you see that all of the Whites who were turned down for a particular internal job opening have more education, better civil service test scores, more work experience and the like than the Blacks who were actually given the jobs, you can be sure that something of an illegal, discriminatory, but highly covert, nature is going on. You are free to pass judgment on these activities, talk about it whenever you feel like doing so and free to talk with a lawyer about what you think. You are also free to join with other Whites who feel they have been injured and pursue the legal redress of your mutual grievances.

Admission to public universities is regulated by a variety of state laws. Color-blind admission usually involves an exclusive reliance on grades and test scores. Racial discrimination occurs when Blacks with low grades and test scores are admitted in preference to Whites with higher grades and test scores. Situations involving public-sector jobs regulated by civil service test scores are similar in nature. Discrimination against Whites is illegal, and the Blacks involved always seem to be unable and unwilling to explain how it happened.

Anti-White discrimination is hard to detect while it is going on in the university admission office or human resources department, but the results are quite easy to detect when you use your eyeballs. If experienced Whites are repeatedly asked to clean up messes left in the wake of the hiring of inexperienced Blacks who do not have the usual qualifications known to be needed to perform the work, such as a certain number of years of experience doing a particular job, you can be sure that some sort of illegal anti-White discrimination is going on somewhere during the hiring process. You never see inexperienced or uneducated lower-class Whites brought in as part of such discriminatory processes, only inexperienced lower-class Blacks.

Blacks who work in white-collar office positions do not keep their jobs for very long if they exhibit violent tendencies. If they grew up the ghetto, they either unlearn how to talk and act as they did in the ghetto or they do not last very long in the white-collar world, where nuance and subtlety are crucial factors for job retention and advancement. The most common specific forms of Black racism in the white-collar world are a covert dislike for having Whites around and practicing illegal covert racism and discrimination that targets Whites. These activities are hard to detect because they are observed only by the perpetrators and are observed only later on by their White victims.

Blacks who work in corporate human resources departments, also known as the personnel department, typically screen employment applications, interview job applicants, make decisions about who to hire and similar activities. Human resources departments screen job applicants by examining their job applications and conducting job interviews.

If a company advertises that they are looking for somebody with a certain number of years of a particular type of work experience, they specifically mention those requirements in their job advertisements. However, if they receive a big pile of applications where a large number of applicants are more or less equal, they can just happen to bring in a pool of applicants of whom most, or all, just happen to be Black. They are required by law to give equal consideration to Whites, but it is rare for anybody to monitor what they do when they those employment applications. They are free to play racial favorites, and you are free to talk about your suspicions about this whenever you feel like it, and pursue legal options if you are so inclined.

Black racists routinely bring up equal opportunity, but are fast to back off from, and block, any sort of situation that involves an open, public, one-on-one comparison with Whites on the basis of objective factors such as standardized civil service test scores and numerical grades. They deny equal opportunity to Whites by blocking open, public, one-on-one comparisons between Blacks and Whites. You are free to talk about this whenever you feel like it. The same applies to college admissions.

If you have filled out employment applications, or been hired into a new job, in recent years, you may have noticed bizarre questions that have appeared on employment applications, and may also have been asked to fill out similarly bizarre checklists as part of the employment process. The bizarre questions concern matters such as whether you have ever been on various types of public assistance and other things that middle-class White people are unlikely to know much about. Such questions are used by companies to bring in certain types of people. Companies receive generous tax credits for hiring habitually unemployed lower-class people with histories of having been on public assistance and related activities.

Nobody has ever demonstrated that having such a background is in any way related to the ability to do the work. You are not eligible for a tax credit for having to put up with such people in your workplace, meaning do their work for them when they take their time coming back from breaks and make a mess of your workplace. That sort of thing happens a lot when people with tangential prior connections to the work force arrive in the workplace. Incidentally, don't be surprised if the people who were hired on the basis of tax-credit criteria come to work hung over.

You are free to write to the company's board of directors about any problems you see going on in your workplace. You are also free to write to them in a manner just as anonymous as was the case for the completely anonymous selection process that inflicted inexperienced applicants with no work ethic on your workplace. You have the same rights as the personnel department to be just as anonymous as they have chosen to be.

This form of Black racism is evidence of a lack of respect for Whites.

The Fifth Type Of Black Racism

The fifth type of Black racism is outright hate speech that does not involve violence or threats of violence. It is common to hear certain types of Black racists use specific racially derogatory hate speech terms such as "Whitey," "cracker," "honky," "redneck" or similar terms when speaking about Whites with other Blacks. You don't have to like it, and you don't have to get used to it either.

Some Black racists don't care whether or not Whites are forced to listen to Blacks using such racially derogatory words on public transit, in the cafeteria or other parts of the workplace because the human resources department will almost never punish such activities when Blacks are the perpetrators. Whites are routinely terminated for saying the same sort of things by Blacks who work in the personnel department who believe that Blacks are entitled to do and say things that Whites are not. Blacks who use racially derogatory speech in the workplace should be put on the fast track for termination from work.

This form of Black racism is evidence of a lack of respect for Whites.

The Sixth Type Of Black Racism

The sixth type of Black racism is the use of racist language as part of a specific demand directed against, or spoken directly to, specific individual Whites on the street or the workplace, often as part of a street beggar routine.

It is common in the Black community to encounter beggars who, like the youth in the old story who cried wolf at every turn, claim to see the White wolf of racism every minute of every day. Such bogus wailing about racism is manufactured for the consumption of Whites who are unable to avoid being forced to listen to such wailing, often as a prelude for a high-volume demand for money.

Middle-class Blacks who stay in school and hold steady jobs have little use for the sort of high-school dropouts who live in relatives' basements, never seem to find jobs and claim that Whites won't let them get ahead because they are Black and poor. This is a ghetto con game perpetrated by street beggars and other semi-criminal frauds.

Examples include saying things such as telling Whites that it is "racist" for Whites to not give money to the sort of street beggars who demands "spare change," and saying that Whites "owe" Black something because of the supposed "legacy of slavery."

Some people don't like to work for a living, and claim that "Whitey" is responsible for their unemployment. This is no different than a White alcoholic with a long list of air-tight, but fictitious, excuses why everybody has it in for him, when the truth is that his alcoholism is the one and only culprit.

This form of Black racism is evidence of a lack of respect for Whites.

The Seventh Type Of Black Racism

The seventh type of Black racism involves making false charges of racism against Whites.

Many, though not all, Black racists of the sort who falsely charge Whites with racism are criminals from the ghetto. Hatred and envy of Whites are considered normal behavior in the ghetto, though very few Whites are to be found available to be hated in the ghetto. When such Black racists get the chance to abuse real-life Whites, they wait until no White witnesses are around and then go on to claim that the White individual in their vicinity said or did something of a racist nature.

Such Black racists are usually habitual criminals, drug addicts, alcoholics or jealous losers who cannot stand being near someone who has done better than they have. A Black racist who works on the loading dock after dropping out of high school with a White college student during the summer may resent the fact that the White is in college. When a single White individual is the only White present in a wolf-pack group of Black racist felons, the felons are likely to decide to victimize him because it is the nature of habitual criminals to do such thing to Whites. Felons are not charitable Samaritans.

Felons lie for a living when they are not busy committing crimes for a living, so you can be absolutely sure that anyone who has a couple of felonies wound up in prison because he has no education or work ethic worthy of the name. If he did, he would have finished high school, gotten a job and veered away from committing crimes.

If you have the misfortune to work with one or more such psychopathic felons, do not say anything at all when their lies induce the personnel department to pull you in for a discussion. Make a non-negotiable demand that whatever the Black racist felon said against you be put in writing and be signed, and then obtain a copy.

Always be sure to get their names. After you get their names, feel free to contact the police and your own lawyer. You may find out that the Black racist who made false charges against you has a warrant out for his arrest, is a chronic alcoholic and drunk driver, drunk driver or has some other such problem.

This form of Black racism is evidence of a lack of respect for Whites.

The Eighth Type Of Black Racism

The eighth type of Black racism is the sexual exploitation of White women. This includes dumping

White women after they become pregnant and failing to pay child support.

Racist Black men can often be seen pursuing, or being involved with, White women. The reason is quite simple. They look down on White men because they stay in school, work for a living, stay out or prison, and so on. Whatever the White man has, other than education, a work ethic and a long-term vision for the future, the Black racist wants it, but does not want to work or study for it. Ghetto culture teaches them to not work for a living if there is any way to get away with it.

However, their hatred for all things White ends where their envy for the White man's "possessions" begins, which includes White women. Black racists see women of all races as possessions.

They seek out White women for relationships, not necessarily because the White women in question are attractive or compatible, but simply because they are White, which is a form of racism.

The Black racist thinks he has triumphed when he gets his hands on one of the White man's supposed "possessions," a notion which would be news to White women. Many Blacks and Whites have commented that the sort of White women they see gallivanting with lower-class Black men look like they come from the lower social classes. Racist Black men and their White female companions often come from the low end of the social class spectrum.

Relationships whose sole motivation is the Black man's desire to get his hands on something that he thinks the White man values have no basis for anything beyond an exploitative overnight relationship.

Since people in such relationships are not compatible, they often do not stay together for very long. Over half of all Black children are born out of wedlock, and a similar ratio probably applies to children born out of Black male Racist-White female relationships.

Black racists take no responsibility for their actions, including child support and even showing up in the delivery room to sign the birth certificate. Black racists consider themselves unaccountable for their actions, at least until court orders compel them to pay child support. Black racists are not adult males for the reason that they do few of the things that adult men do, such as supporting the families they bring into being.

This form of Black racism is evidence of a lack of respect for Whites.

The Ninth Type Of Black Racism

The ninth type of Black racism is the use of violence and threats of violence, meaning felony intimidation threats specifically directed against Whites, usually by Black career criminals who are also racists.

Black racists usually start committing crimes against Whites early in life as part of their criminal careers. They begin with activities such as robbing younger Whites in grade school and graduate to more serious violent crimes before dropping out of high school.
Wolf packs of Black racists gang members cruise through White neighborhoods in old cars looking for targets against whom to perpetrate crimes such as theft, home invasion, rape, homicide and various other crimes of violent crimes.

Violent Black-on-White crime can also occur in the workplace, and you can be sure that any Black racist who attacks a White will later say things such as "he had it coming" or "I didn't mean it" or "he's a racist and deserved it" and similar lies of the sort that professional criminals routinely use to describe their victims. Their fellow Black felon racists will routinely deny that anything of a criminal nature ever happened.

The one and only form of respect a White owes Black racist criminals is to spell their names correctly when filing criminal charges or civil lawsuits against them.

This form of Black racism is evidence of a lack of respect for Whites.

The Tenth Type Of Black Racism

The tenth type of Black racism involves denying the existence of racism that has been perpetrated by Blacks against Whites exists at all, including cases where those doing the denying are actually the perpetrators. Such Black racists might deny that a particular event, be it employment discrimination, verbal racism or violent criminal racism perpetrated against one or more White individuals, ever occurred in the first place. This means that they saw or heard something of an illegal nature, or did something, and deny that it happened. Denial of the truth constitutes racism.

This might take the form of a blanket statement that that no Black that ever lived, including themselves, ever engaged in racism. It might involve simply saying nothing when a White is falsely accused of racism by one of their associates on the job. Many other forms of Black-on-White racism are possible, and Whites are victims.

No matter what they did or observed, you will find that they invariably lie by saying that it didn't happen or that the White person or persons involved are racists who are out to get Blacks. They even say this sort of thing when they are caught on camera committing their offenses.

Whatever the details, Black racists see no evil, hear no evil and speak no evil as far as Blacks are concerned. They do so because they hate and envy Whites on some level. They refuse to do the right thing because "anything goes" where Whites are concerned. If a White were to do the same thing to a Black, all of a sudden they would turn out to have photographic memories and be the first to complain.

Twenty to fifty percent of all Blacks are racists who engage in various sorts of racist behavior, including criminal violence directed against Whites. Look at the Black-on-White crime statistics. Many Black-on-White crime perpetrators specifically seek out Whites as their crime victims, which is why such crimes occur in White neighborhoods far from the ghetto residences of the career criminal perpetrators.

This form of Black racism is evidence of a lack of respect for Whites.

Chapter Three
Blacks Who Identify With The Aggressor

Chapter Three
Blacks Who Identify With The Aggressor

Identification With The Aggressor

The "Stockholm Syndrome" is a well-known psychological problem that occurs in people who have been captured and held as involuntary hostages for prolonged periods of time. After being held captive for a period of time, they gradually become sympathetic to their captors. After being released from captivity, some actually take the side of their captors to the extent of speaking out in their favor. Other types of people are known to sympathize with the aggressors, including certain types of Blacks who can be found all social classes.

According to Anna Freud, identification with the aggressor is a psychological problem which involves somebody, male or female, choosing to mentally put themselves in the place of some other person who engages in unprovoked verbal or physical aggression against one or more other people. Identification with the aggressor allows them to sympathize with the aggressors instead of the victims, and they choose to do this deliberately. As time goes on, the possibility of imitative behavior by those who identify with the aggressor increases.

Identification with the aggressor is a syndrome that often occurs among those who vicariously wish they could become aggressors. It also occurs among those who think of aggressors as being people who are worthy of their emulation while falling short of being willing to become aggressors themselves because becoming an aggressor would open them to the risk of being caught and punished.

Identifying with the aggressor involves seeing the world from the viewpoint of the aggressor and actively agreeing with that viewpoint. People who do this deliberately choose to not identify with the victims of the aggressors, or even think about them, because identifying with the aggressor involves disregarding the welfare of the victims of the aggressor.

They instead choose to cheer on aggressors such as bullies and crime perpetrators, which should automatically induce potential victims to categorize them as potentially dangerous. Identification with the aggressor will often lead to the imitation of aggressor behavior. This can lead to the potentially dangerous imitator becoming a truly dangerous aggressor.

Aggressors express their aggression verbally in the form of threats or demands, make use of gestures and body language, and make their aggression known by means of physical violence. Those who identify with the aggressors typically stay on the sidelines and cheer them on, or at least do not express any form of outwardly observable disapproval. This can change over time as they switch over completely to the aggressor's viewpoint.

Black racists who identify with Black aggressors typically say something to the effect that the White victims had it coming to them or some other such fraudulent statement founded on their underlying sympathy for the aggressor. There is nothing positive about emotional sympathy with criminals, and those who do so deserve no respect.

As time goes on, Blacks who identify with the aggressor may choose to become personally and physically involved in imitating and thereby perpetrating Black racism against Whites, particularly if they think that they can get away with avoiding getting caught and being punished.

Blacks and Whites who identify with the aggressor see the world from the aggressor's point of view and believe whatever the aggressors say, no matter how untruthful it might be. They simply pretend that it is true even when the evidence says that it is not true. If they benefit personally from committing crimes, they claim that they are just having a little fun.

Some Whites are uneasy about being White and do not identify with other Whites. Such Whites sometimes identify with Black aggressors, because they identify with, and express support for, Black racists. This might include Whites who might be on the receiving end of minor forms of Black racism, such as Whites who work in human resources departments.

In the white-collar world of a human resources department, a White employee might see subtle signs that those who disagree with the prevailing ideology to the effect that Blacks are entitled to discriminate against Whites are routinely terminated.

If such Whites express dissent from the party line, they may soon lose their jobs for failing to exhibit a constructive team attitude on a team where anti-White discrimination is the party line. Whites facing possible job loss will often mentally change sides and identify with the aggressor. Aggressors and people who identify with aggressors are not your friends, so do not think of them as your friends, particularly if they have any sort of power over you.

Identification With Criminal Aggressors

If a Black thief robs several people, and most of the victims are Whites who live in neighborhoods some distance from the Black thief's residence, that Black criminal thief is a Black racist because he goes out of his way to target Whites as his victims. The Black thief probably cruises in White neighborhoods because he sees them as productive hunting grounds for thieves such as himself.

Attacks against Whites perpetrated by Blacks in cases where the Whites who were attacked have reason to believe that race is a motivational factor in their having been attacked constitutes racism. It is the victim's opinion that counts, not the perpetrators opinions or the opinions of apologists who identify with the perpetrators. Courts exist to settle such disputes

Criminals always deny both their criminal activities and their motivations. In such cases, the opinions of the victims of Black racists take precedence over the opinions of both the Black racists and the opinions of the apologists for Black racists who identify with the aggressor. Black racism is both anti-White and anti-victim in nature.

Blacks who say it is racist to mention that Blacks target Whites for crimes are themselves outright Black racists. Court records show that Blacks routinely target Whites for crimes. If a million Black racists misrepresent something, it remains untrue. The burden of proof is always on the person who makes a claim. Blacks who identify with career criminals and their interests should be considered to be potentially dangerous.

Chapter Four
The Secret History Of Black Racism

Chapter Four
The Secret History
Of Black Racism

How Black Racism Developed

White European peasants were held as serfs for over a thousand years. However, Whites of European descent do not claim that they can't get ahead in the modern world due to the White race's psychological legacy of serfdom. They just get on with their lives.

A lot of Blacks seem to have trouble getting on with their lives because they either live in the past or claim to be unable to move on. Black racists routinely bring up the "legacy of slavery" issue as their all-purpose excuse for every educational and vocational problem they bring down upon themselves by dropping out of school and choosing to become career criminals. Black racists dwell on the topic of slavery for covert reasons they never talk about but which Whites are free to analyze.

During the slavery era, if a plantation slave stole something, and nobody confessed, all of the slaves on that plantation were punished by means such as depriving all of them of a meal. Black slaves did not want to point out the thief because they had to work alongside the thief for the rest of their lives and could expect to be subjected to retaliation. Even if they had no love whatsoever for the thief on the personal level, they were not interested in inspiring retaliation from people they had to see every day. Contemporary Black criminals do much the same thing: they have a group mentality that guides their behavior.

This was one point of origin of the Black group identity, in the sense of a folk tradition that evolved into a group consensus about what sorts of ethnocentric behavior were acceptable and not acceptable for Blacks. Blacks stuck together and presented a united front when dealing with White and Black plantation overseers. The contemporary end result is that many ghetto Blacks do not consider it socially acceptable for Blacks to point out Black criminal behavior to Whites, or even admit that Blacks commit crimes against Whites. They stick together because that is the modern-day group consensus they evolved over time.

This ethnocentric group consensus is one form of legitimization of Black racist crimes against contemporary Whites, because Black folk traditions marginalized Whites as a group as being evil slave-owners and overseers. Some contemporary ghetto Blacks thus choose to close ranks when they perceive White outsiders daring to criticize, or punish, Blacks for everyday Black ghetto behavior such as murder, theft and rape. Some middle-class suburban Blacks who do not live in ghettos also do this, but act quite differently when they are the ones who are attacked by ghetto Blacks.

Black Slave Owners, Overseers And Slave-Drivers

Contemporary Black racists never mention that Blacks once owned other Blacks as their personal slaves. Blacks also worked as plantation overseers and as slave-drivers, sometimes working for White slave-owners and sometimes working for Black slave-owners. Overseers were the general managers of large plantations with more than twenty-five slaves. Slave-drivers, or drivers, were the foremen, or immediate supervisors, of groups of slaves on large plantations.

Carter G. Woodson, a Black historian, the author of a book about antebellum Blacks who were slave-owners, noted that about one out of seven Blacks had been freed before the Emancipation Proclamation, and about half of all Southern Whites did not own slaves. Harriet Beecher Stowe wrote that plantation slaves invariably became tyrants whenever they got the opportunity to do so, and noted that Blacks who became overseers of other Blacks on plantations were inevitably more tyrannical than White overseers. Kenneth Stampp noted that Black slave-drivers were often given better clothing than the other field slaves. Overseers and slave-drivers were usually the parties who personally administered whippings to slaves. Blacks thus played supporting roles in slavery that few contemporary Blacks will acknowledge. Contemporary Blacks also do not care to acknowledge that parts of this legacy continue to live on in the folk traditions that have been maintained by contemporary Blacks in the context of contemporary ghetto culture.

Black overseers and Black slave-drivers internalized the psychological viewpoints of White slave-owners and White overseers. They identified with the aggressor, which means that they chose to imitate the aggressors in their thoughts and actions. They chose to adopt a more intensified version of the White overseer mentality than was the case among White overseers and slave-owners, most likely because Black overseers and Black slave-drivers did not have the option of leaving their jobs that the White overseers and White slave-drivers had. They thus did anything and everything they could to hold onto their jobs, which elevated them a few steps above the other plantation slaves. People in every era are capable of putting their own self-interest above the interests of others, and Blacks are no exception.

When someone takes on another person's point of view, they identify with that other person, in the sense of seeing the world as that other person does, and often use it as the basis for imitation. They imitate aggressors in word and deed because they want to be like them.

Identification With The Overseer

After slavery ended, Blacks who had worked as overseers and slave-drivers had nowhere to go but the community of freedmen. They had a great deal of practice being overseers and slave-drivers, and probably did not know how to do anything else, because they had no skills other than those related to controlling and abusing other people. The end result was that some Black former overseers and slave-drivers continued to behave and think as they had during the slavery era.

Former overseers and slave-drivers continued to imitate the elements of the slavery system that had benefited them personally during the slavery era, meaning bullying, controlling and attacking people. It is not much of a step from being a slave-driver or overseer to becoming a post-slavery local bully or criminal who beat up, robbed and attacked others. Some probably became criminal gang members after the Civil War.

Certain aspects of the plantation mentality and social system survived after slavery ended among Blacks because some of the Blacks who had worked as overseers and slave-drivers chose to maintain the folk traditions of the overseer and slave-driver. Their folk tradition was an oral tradition of the plantation social system where some Blacks were overseers and others were their subordinate underlings.

Poor Blacks who went on to live in ghettos developed the sort of neighborhood social structure that people with no tradition of formal learning could be expected to have, given that their primary source of knowledge was orally-transmitted folk traditions: they continued to act out certain elements of the plantation and sharecropper systems with those who had previously acted out the roles of Black overseers and Black slave-drivers emerging as post-slavery local tyrants and criminals.

There are substantial behavioral similarities and parallels between contemporary ghetto criminal behavior and plantation overseer behavior.

Ghetto criminals routinely threaten to beat anyone who does not obey them, a custom which originated on the plantation, though prison experiences may also play a role in reinforcing this sort of overseer-style behavior.

Ghetto culture discourages formal education, which was also the case on plantations. In the absence of formal education, the only things that ghetto residents will grow up learning about will be oral folk traditions passed down and imitated by the descendants of overseers and slave-drivers. There is no other possible source for such practices other than the oral traditions of people without formal education. Overseers and slave-drivers have no parallels in modern-day White culture except in prisons, so this sort of behavior is unlikely to have been transmitted to contemporary Blacks by Whites. Blacks themselves are responsible.

Ghettos As Plantations

Contemporary Blacks who bring up the "legacy of slavery" are talking about the elements of the slavery-plantation system that Blacks themselves continue to keep alive in the specific form of a rigid hierarchical ghetto caste system where violent criminals are the neighborhood overseers and slave-drivers, and anybody they choose to designate must obey them or face a beating or worse.

They talk about the legacy of slavery because they see it in action in the ghetto every day. Everybody talks about Black gangs and violence without explicitly mentioning that gangs are simply modern-day extensions of the Black overseer and slave-driver system passed down by Blacks from the slavery era and mimicked by contemporary Blacks.

The lack of respect for formal education in the ghetto I also a psychological relic of the plantation mentality that continues to be perpetuated by contemporary

Blacks. Overseers and slave-drivers were not noted for their educational prowess, and have no interest in seeing local potential victims become educated and leave the ghettos, the last thing contemporary Black criminal overseers and slave-drivers want to happen. Blacks learn to drop out of school from contemporary Blacks in the ghettos just as they learn to become criminals from contemporary Blacks. They identify with and mimic the overseer social role.

Disrespect for work is a plantation slave folk tradition that lives on in modern-day ghettos full of uneducated people who look down on formal education. Slaves often engaged in tactics such as work slowdowns that were intended to thwart the slave owners' efforts to get as much work as possible out of them. This is a folk tradition maintained by American Blacks exclusively. Foreign-born blacks who live in American ghettos avoid picking up this tradition just they avoid dropping out of school. They recognize it as a cultural tradition that leads nowhere.

This folk tradition is counterproductive in modern societies where people must work for a living, a notion that most ghetto dropouts do not seem to have acquired. Someone who refuses to stay in school is unwelcome in the modern-day job market, and is even more unwelcome when their attitude radiates disrespect for the idea of working for a living in general.

Black criminals share this disrespect for work. They believe they are entitled to live without working and feel that entitled to be free to attack whoever they want whenever they want. They attack crime witnesses and victims who disobey their commands, and in doing so they mimic plantation overseers and slave drivers. They claim to hate the legacy of slavery but the truth is that they work at mimicking what they claim to hate so much because being criminals is the only thing they are willing to do.

There is another plantation role that Black racists seek out and emulate: the role of breeder. Male slaves with certain qualities were often bred with female slaves to produce offspring with those characteristics. Some breeders were rented by slave owners and moved around from one plantation to another. It's easy to see a contemporary street dude acting out such a role. Both Racist and non-racist Black men idolize the role of breeder.

Various common types of ghetto behavior, such as alcoholism, illegitimacy, absentee fathers, lack of a work ethic, disregard for education and other types of aberrant behavior are simply folk-tradition remnants of the plantation mentality that have been passed down through the generations in the form of oral traditions by Blacks to other Blacks. There are no contemporary models in White society that can account for such behavior, least of all among people who disdain formal education.

Ghetto violence also perpetuates the plantation social caste mentality. Violent ghetto criminals act as overseers when they commit crimes and administer beatings. The idolization of violence by ghetto Blacks is part of a way of life that perpetuates the Black overseer mentality as the centerpiece of ghetto life. Black drug dealers, pimps and so on are simply thinly-veiled contemporary adaptations of the role of Black overseer that have been taken up by modern-day criminals who are actually imitating their great-grandfathers' overseers and slave-drivers. Sadistic crime is the common in the ghetto because ghetto gang members choose to imitate the folk tradition of sadistic overseers. There is no other possible modern-day cultural source for this folk tradition, and it has no parallel in modern-day White society.

There is no meaningful difference between a sadistic Black drug dealer walking around attacking anybody he feels like attacking and a Black plantation overseer walking whipping people. Both types control people with violence and threats. Black racists enjoy acting out the social roles of slave owners, slave drivers and overseers, and see Asians, foreign-born Blacks, Whites, and Blacks who act "White," as their potential victims. It is not hard to see the desire the control Whites and their property as a motivating force among such Black racists, many of whom probably fantasize about running a plantation with Whites as slaves. Ghetto culture thus combines the folk traditions of historical plantation slavery and contemporary racist overseer-style criminal behavior, and directs it against Whites, foreign-born Blacks, Asians and Blacks who act "White" as well as anybody that happens to be living in the ghetto.

Street males often say that they demand that the world respect them, but they refuse to respect others. This sounds a lot like an overseer demanding that he be respected administering whippings. Street males start to get ready for lives of street crime at an early age because street criminals are the only people on their neighborhoods they see doing well in monetary terms.

Very few Black professionals choose to live in violence-prone ghettos over the suburbs, so the absence of adult male role models in ghettos is not surprising. In suburban schools, adolescents are educated to develop skills that will help them get into colleges and skills that will help them in the job market. In the ghetto, up-and-coming Black criminals acquire the sort of informal skills that lead to the local criminal activities "job market." People are shaped by their environments, and the ghetto is no exception.

One peculiarity about Black racist criminals is that although they disrespect their middle-class White crime victims, they often spend whatever money they obtain by crooked means on lower-class versions of what they see on television: ridiculously big, chrome-plated cars, gold jewelry for men, expensive but trashy clothing and high-priced liquor. Such activities reveal how their social class filters what they see on television into ghetto version of the White middle-class world. They want what the White world offers consumers, but customize it to reflect their lower-class tastes.

The patterns of the lives they lead are inevitably lower-class in nature. It is common for street males who accumulate large amounts of money to die of completely avoidable diseases such as lung cancer brought on by smoking, cancer brought on by high-fat diets and alcoholism-induced kidney failure. As the twig is bent, so is the tree inclined.

Chapter Five
Blacks Who Pretend That Black Racism Does Not Exist

Chapter Five
Blacks Who Pretend That Black Racism Does Not Exist

Blacks Who Identify With Slave-Owners

Machiavelli wrote that we never know the whole truth about the past. Slavery was known as the "peculiar institution" in the antebellum South in part because many Southerners were of the peculiar opinion that the issue of slavery was not debatable. Slavery was the economic basis of the South, and those who benefited from slavery, meaning parties such as slave-owners and overseers, were disinclined to discuss or defend the institution of slavery when confronted with outsiders.

Charles MacKay visited the antebellum South and wrote about how Southerners adamantly refused to discuss slavery: "The South…. forbids the expression of opinion on this subject. No doubt it would be dangerous to allow of free discussion…..it is not to be supposed that those who are educated in the belief that they profit by it can do otherwise, than forbid, within their own jurisdiction, the calling of it into question…… thought was not free."

People who benefit from any sort of laws, economic institutions, preferential treatment and similar types of arrangements often consider such arrangements to be the indisputable and unchangeable natural order of the universe, and therefore forbid inquiries, criticisms and debates. This is exactly what the slave-owners did. John Locke wrote that "men espouse opinions that best comport with their power, profit, or credit, and then seek arguments to support them." It would hardly be surprising that some Blacks became aware of the beliefs and attitudes held by the slave-owners on whose plantations they spent their lives. Folk traditions concerning such beliefs and attitudes survived and appear to have been adopted by contemporary Blacks who identify with the aggressor.

Black racists espouse predictable rationalizations about the subject of Black racism that are remarkably similar to the rationalizations for slavery held in the antebellum South. Black racists claim that Black racism does not exist because they refuse discuss or consider the issue, which is reminiscent of an ostrich whose head is stuck in the sand. This is a typical example of identification with the aggressor in the sense of mimicking arguments promulgated by antebellum Southern slave-owners while denying that any such thing is going on.

People who identify with an aggressor not only will not admit that they identify with the aggressor, they will also do everything they can to block discussion and analysis of the fact that they identify with the aggressor, particularly among the victims and potential victims of aggressors. People who benefit from something illicit do not want anyone finding out about the skeletons hidden in their closets. Black racists do and say whatever is in their own self-interest without regard for the truth or the interests of other people.

John Locke wrote that "It is not evidence he seeks, but the quiet enjoyment of the opinion he is fond of, with a forward condemnation of all that may stand in opposition to it, unheard and unexamined; which, what is it but prejudice?" In the case of Black racists, outright prejudice against Whites and their interests is the driving motivation behind their desire to have the issue of Black racism remain a superstitiously taboo subject for Whites. Whites do not benefit from being told to close their minds, so they should do exactly what they have been told to avoid, and let the chips fall where they may.

More precisely, their problem is what John Stuart Mill termed interest-begotten prejudice, which occurs when "any set of persons who mix much together, and have a common interest, are apt to make that common interest their standard of virtue." There are numerous Blacks who have benefitted from discrimination against Whites and have accumulated college admissions letters, civil service promotions and on-the-job promotions that would otherwise have gone to more qualified Whites were objective criteria such as test scores to be the only criteria to be used. Their business in life is to profit from discrimination and other forms of anti-White activities.

Those who benefit from discrimination never bring up what happens to the Whites whose places they took on the job and in school. The particular prejudiced interest they have in common is pretending that discrimination against Whites never takes place and that they are somehow morally superior because they took the place of Whites. This form of over-emphasis is common among wrong-doers. Naturally they do not want Whites, or anybody else, for that matter, enquiring too closely into exactly how they got to where they are, meaning by walking all over other people and their interests.

Some Blacks thus benefit from forbidding or blocking discussion of Black racism because it helps fend off inquiries and legal responses by victims. Saying that the issue of Black racism, and the effects of Black racism on Whites, cannot be discussed or critically examined by Whites are guilty of either identifying with antebellum aggressors or of attempting to manipulate Whites into accepting the bogus premise that Black racists decide what Whites can and cannot talk and think about.

Either way, they are racists. If there is an alternative explanation, they are welcome to make it public, and are not welcome to pretend that the issue does not exist.

The principle of forbidding the expression of opinion on this subject is a common criminal tactic used to intimidate witnesses from talking or thinking about crimes and criminals.

It also sounds similar to a religious dogma such that believers claim cannot be challenged or examined by anyone because they happen to believe it should never be challenged.

Many Blacks have personally profited from discrimination against Whites, meaning those who were admitted to colleges in preference to Whites with higher grades and test scores, and those who were hired under illegal racial quota systems. They are quite aware that they have taken the places of better-qualified Whites. They simply pretend to not be aware of this.

Upton Sinclair said that it is difficult to get a man to understand something when his job depends on not understanding it. Black racists understand perfectly well that they are the beneficiaries of Black-on-White racism, and are not inclined to admit it, dwell on it, or want to have Whites to do so. They pretend that the issue does not exist, pretend that that they do not understand the question, tell Whites to not discuss the issue or change the subject.

Free Speech And The Conspiracy Of Silence

Free speech has a long history. William Blackstone summarized British common law when he wrote that "Every freeman has an undoubted right to lay what sentiments he pleases before the public; to forbid this is to destroy the freedom of the press." The trial of John Peter Zenger was one of the factors that led to the founding of the United States. His trial established that free and open discussion of unpalatable truths was not libel, no matter how much damage the public revelation of the truth did to the perpetrators of wrongdoing. Zenger himself wrote that "No nation ancient or modern ever lost the liberty of freely speaking, writing, or publishing their sentiments, but forthwith lost their liberty in general and became slaves."

One basic military principle is that the best generals are those who can get their enemies to lay down their arms without a fight. This is a standard tactic of Black racist criminals: attempting to get Whites to agree with the fraudulent beliefs that Black racism does not exist and is an issue that should not be discussed or investigated by Whites. Telling Whites they "owe" something to Blacks because of the "legacy of slavery" is simply a form of ghetto fraud perpetrated by Black racists.

Black racist who don't like what Whites say or write should leave the premises. Whites do not have to stop talking or writing about things because Black racists dislike having Black racism brought up. A 1931 US Supreme court case, Near v. Minnesota, 283 U.S. 697 affirmed that prior restraint of speech or writing is illegal and unconstitutional. The issues of Black racism and the effects of Black racism are always open for discussion by Whites, particularly the White victims of Black racism.

Whites can demand reasons, proof, and evidence of anyone on any issue, and are similarly free to disregard those whose claims are unsupported by, or contrary to, what the evidence states to be reality. Black racists are peculiarly deficient both in providing evidence to support their claims regarding the nonexistence of Black racism and explaining why they dismiss Black-on-White crime statistics and court decisions that have found discrimination against Whites to be illegal. John Locke wrote that "There cannot any one moral rule be proposed, whereof a man may not justly demand a reason."

Black racists claim that their actions are not racist or discriminatory because "everyone knows" that Blacks are supposedly incapable of discrimination or racism. If they are telling the truth, it should be incredibly easy for them to prove what they claim "everyone knows", but no proof is forthcoming because they are lying. The burden of proof is always on those who make claims. Whites do not have to disprove what has never been proven in the first place. Black racists who are deficient in providing proof and reasons to support their claims should always be assumed to be liars until proof to the contrary is brought forth.

The Immorality Of Black Racists

Understanding that Black racism does not benefit Whites is the starting point for analyzing, and passing judgment on, Black racism. Black racism demands that Whites sacrifice their self-interests with nothing being offered in return. When people lie to you, or deny that your personal experience with Black racism are valid, you can react to them in the manner of your choosing.

Blacks like to say that you can do anything if you are White. Take them at their word. Literally. Step on the toes of Black racists by contradicting them at every turn. You do not have to care what they think. Opinions are fluff, and the opinions of Black racists and their supporters have no more intellectual weight than dandelion seeds carried aloft in the summer air. You have the same rights as they do.

John Locke wrote that "False and doubtful positions, relied upon as unquestionable maxims, keep those who build on them in the dark from truth. Such are usually the prejudices imbibed from education, party, reverence, fashion interest, et cetera." People who seek power over others often attempt to obtain such power by getting others to accept bogus premises without critical analysis and then go on to take something of value from them. Do not allow Black racists to mislead you by taking anything they say on blind faith.

When people cannot get what they want by direct means, they attempt to get what they want by telling lies. People of all races tell lies to advance their personal and group interests, including Blacks. Fabricating a system of morality that applies only to Whites, meaning a double standard of morality, is a form of lying. Black racists espouse a particular definition of morality that just happens to benefit Blacks by virtue of blaming Whites and pretending that Blacks are always innocent of wrongdoing. Black racists developed this this moralistic viewpoint in order to help themselves acquire power and social status by deceiving and manipulating Whites.

All of the talk about Whites "owing" Blacks for slavery is just a means towards the end of obtaining what they cannot obtain by merit and work. It is form of opportunistic begging. Pretending that Black-on-White crime does not exist is one way they attempt to get Whites to give into them. Whites who laugh at their demands are routinely charged with being racists because that is what career criminals do.

Black racists don't respect their victims in general and go out of their way to disrespect Whites in particular because they don't like having prospective victims refusing to be victimized or be subjected to lies by beggars with a menacing air about them.

They offer no evidence or proof, only dogmatic lies masquerading as facts, and Black racists who spout such dogmas are prejudiced against Whites. There is thus no reason for Whites to pretend that Black racists are telling the truth or to take them seriously. Most Black racists are career criminals, and career criminals demand that their victims respect them for lying. There is no reason to respect Black racists who lie to you, and plenty of reasons to not respect Black racists who lie to you. Liars deserve nothing.

Chapter Six
Ghetto Racism

Chapter Six
Ghetto Racism

Ghettos And Ethnocentricity

Ghettos are places where large numbers of poor people live in close proximity to each other, often in rundown housing. There are White ghettos, Asian ghettos and Black ghettos where people of the same race, culture, or both, can be found.

When people of the same race or ethnicity live together, their character structure tends to conform to a pattern. Ethnocentricity is one part of this, and involves seeing one's own race or culture as being the center of everything. Black ethnocentricity induces ghetto Blacks to exaggerate and intensify everything about themselves which differentiates them from Whites and members of other ethnic groups.

Blacks in ghettos thus speak, think, dress and live differently than suburban Whites, as well as suburban Blacks, because their culture is deliberately intended to be different than White culture. A tight connection between race and culture develops when all of the people in a given area are of the same race or culture, because being around like-minded people tends to reinforce certain types of behavioral tendencies among group members.

The cultural points of differentiation that group members develop serve to induce ghetto Blacks look upon outsiders with contempt. The poorer they are, the more likely they are to see other ethnic, cultural and racial groups in negative terms as a byproduct of envy of those who have more than they do, and the more likely they are to see their own ethnic group as being important.

Ethnocentric beliefs lead Black ghetto residents to demand that all Blacks should conform to, help defend, whatever the behavioral consensus might be among local ghetto residents. Those who disagree about conforming are likely to become marginalized, be looked down upon and might even be attacked for failing to support the ghetto party line. Dissenters soon find out that their opinions are unwelcome and that they should not criticize the ghetto consensus on behavior such as criminal activities.

If the ghetto consensus defines crime as "normal" behavior, those who report crimes and defend themselves against criminals will soon find themselves in trouble with unpleasant people in the ghetto. Non-conformists are not welcome. If the ghetto consensus is that education is insufficiently ethnocentric, those who attempt to finish high school may find themselves being attacked on the way to school. Acting different attracts punishment in the ghetto.

When the ghetto behavioral consensus is such that criminal activity is directed against Whites because they are seen as enemies is the social norm, Whites become hated, envied and preyed upon, education is laughed at because it "White", acting "White" is seen as unforgiveable, and every Black is be expected to help enforce this group consensus. Nonconformists become nonpersons. This is a strictly local form of consensus. In other places, such as an affluent White or Black suburb, such beliefs would be considered intolerable.

Ethnocentricity is the belief that one's own race is the center of everything, and other races should be scaled and rated with reference to one's own race in a negative manner. It leads to Black racists becoming prejudiced because they believe that their ethnic group, or at least that part of the Black race that espouses their beliefs, are more important than any other race or ethnicity, or at least should be.

Black racists are both ethnocentric and xenophobic. Ethnocentricity means that they see their own ethnic group and customs as being superior to all other ethnic groups. Xenophobia means disliking, hating or looking down on outsider ethnic groups simply because they are not one's own ethnic group.

The greater the degree to which an ethnocentric Black sees his own ethnicity as being "superior," the greater the degree to which he is likely to become a racist who treats outsiders, including Whites, with envy and contempt. Whites become marginalized in the ghetto because they are not Black, and this includes White crime victims.

Hatreds arise from fear and envy, as Machiavelli noted. Xenophobic hatred constitutes racism, and Black racism is simply a specific form of xenophobic hatred fueled by the hatred and envy of Whites. Xenophobic hatred on the part of ghetto Blacks is most often directed at Whites, though Asians and even Blacks who talk or act "White" can easily become targets of violence and threats perpetrated by Black racists.

Blacks who look, talk or act like the white enemy will be treated like they are enemies. Lying to Whites about anything an individual Black feels like lying about is socially acceptable among xenophobic Blacks because Whites are hated and envied. Denying the existence of Black racism is part of the xenophobic mentality. Changing the subject is another common tactic used by Blacks who deny the existence of Black racism. This often involves blaming the White victim of an attack by one or more Blacks. If the television news shows a group of Blacks attacking or robbing Whites, Black racists say that the victim had it coming.

Blacks love to bring up the legacy of slavery as their all-purpose excuse for every form of crime and discrimination against Whites. Many Blacks sympathize with the criminals instead of their victims because there is widespread identification with criminal aggressors in ghettos.

Ghettos And Crime

Whites often hear from the mass media about the astronomical unemployment rates in Black ghettos. These statistics, however, simply reflect the observable mainstream parts of the economy. When you factor in the "underground" parts of the economy, meaning the sort of criminal activities that are not included in the formal economic and unemployment statistics, you get a very different picture of the Black ghetto economy where criminals sprout up like weeds.

Most Whites are unaware that a large, difficult-to-measure, but real, percentage of Blacks in the ghetto have never had a real job in the sense of working nine-to-five for a paycheck in a factory, office or other formal organization. The reality is that these supposedly unemployed men and women work full time in underground-economy criminal activity "jobs" of the sort where a single offense can get them put away for many years.

At any given time, about ten percent of all American Black men are incarcerated. About half of all Black men spend some part of their lives in prison, and a large percent of Black men under the age of eighteen have had contact with the criminal justice system in forms such as having a youth worker.

The only time that these career criminals get mainstream jobs is when they are forced into work-release programs towards the end of their prison sentences. Once their work-release programs are over, they return to the same sort of underground-economy things in which they engaged before being locked up.

Black criminals who do not want to take chances on being locked up repeatedly do not stop being criminals after getting out of prison. They simply change their approach to crime to resemble the white-collar criminal approach. They tell lies in an attempt to control other people's money and property. They attempt to talk unsophisticated suckers into investing in bogus enterprises. They attempt to defraud addled widows out of their life savings and similar sorts of scams and hustles. Some also turn to attempting to convince Whites that they owe Blacks a living because of the "legacy of slavery," which is simply a ghetto hustle that targets Whites.

Ghetto residents who are not directly involved in crime in the sense of committing violent crimes such as robberies might be on the fringes of criminal activity. This can happen with ghetto residents who buy stolen property from thieves for cash. The primary form of economic activity that those who grow up in the ghetto hear about most often is not nine-to-five jobs but rather various forms of career criminal activities. Crime is the social norm in the ghetto.

People who either already are, or are on their way to becoming, career criminals, are obsessed with other people respecting them because they are criminals. Ghetto dropouts hate nonconformists who show that they can get ahead in any manner other than criminal activities.

This is why attending high school in the ghetto will get you laughed at and make you a target for attacks because staying in school makes dropouts, who constitute the majority of ghetto residents, look bad by comparison. High school dropout rates of fifty percent and more are common in the ghetto.

Few ghetto residents know anybody with a real career other than in crime, so ghetto residents grow up thinking that finishing high school is a joke. They hear from other ghetto dropouts that they can make money in criminal activities of the sort conducted by gangs. The end result is that ninety-eight percent of the residents of state prisons are gang members who are also ghetto high school dropouts. Dropping out of high school steers the dropout towards winding up either dead by age thirty in a gang war or ending up in the state prison with other dropouts.

Black men and women who drop out of high school have ninety percent of their lives written out in advance for them. The job market doesn't want them because they don't have any skills to offer the job market, and talk and dress in ways that are guaranteed to ensure that they are unwelcome outside the ghetto. Ghetto-style speech and clothing don't go over well in white-collar office environments.

Crime Is A Ghetto Career

Suburban Whites and Blacks who finish high school and college go on to get jobs in offices and factories. Ghetto dropouts are not welcome anywhere in the mainstream economy because they do not have the reading, writing and mathematics skills necessary to compete with those who do have those skills. They turn to crime as a career because that is what everybody around them is doing, and they see few alternatives open to dropouts who lack skills and a work ethic.

Ghetto criminals don't want to hear that crime is bad for victims because they do not identify with their crime victims. They don't want to hear about victim rights that because they don't want anybody opposing their means of self-support. Black racist criminals thus see crime as a career and see potential White crime victims as cannon fodder for their lifestyle.

Envy is common among thieves. If a thief sees something he wants, he becomes envious and initiates criminal violence against his victim for the purpose of relieving his emotional envy by stealing and taking possession of what the other person owns. When Black thieves see what suburban White men have, they become envious because they do not have it, and go on to steal it because they want it, like a hungry wolf spotting a small animal and snatching it for dinner.

A Black racist criminal who targets Whites because he thinks of Whites as opportunistic targets for victimization who will not put up much a fight deserve prison sentences. Committing crimes that target people because of their race is usually considered to be a hate crime, and Black racists deserve prison time for attacking Whites. They have chosen to be dangerous.

Ghetto culture allows career criminals to get away crime, but their victims are not so lucky. Black racist criminals never respect crime victims. White victims thus should never respect those who perpetrate crimes against Whites or discriminate against Whites.

Sometimes blacks help Whites escape attacks initiated by groups of Blacks, and such Samaritans almost always either come from outside the ghetto or are foreign-born blacks who do not subscribe to the premises of ghetto culture.

Ghetto Attitudes Towards Crime

Black men often tell Black women that they are of the opinion that "there are too many Black men in prison already." This is a form of Black-on-Black behavioral expectation used to socially pressure Black women to not file criminal charges against Black men who attack them. Note that this situation involves Black-on-Black crime, with no Whites involved. In this particular case, Black men as a group are the in-group, or insiders, and Black women are the "out-group, or outsiders. Those who do not conform to such the cultural ideals of the ghetto are made to feel socially unwelcome in the ghetto.

Those espousing such opinions do not mention that too many people have been made into crime victims by Black men. If there one Black criminal who is not in prison for his crimes, then there are not enough Black men in prison. Criminals and those who identify with them routinely intimidate and mislead crime victims and witnesses, and this is one way in which they do it. Black racists do similar things to Whites as part of their standard operating procedure for dealing with actual and potential victims and witnesses. Fraud and misrepresentation are tools they use to control other people's thoughts and actions.

A Black murderer who grew up in a Black area once said that violence is as American as cherry pie. He was writing from experience about people such as himself. Black racist crime perpetrators see committing crimes against Whites as being as American as cherry pie as well. The victims of Black racist criminals should thus see pressing criminal charges as being as American as cherry pie as well.

The same principle applies to Whites, Asians and Blacks who act "White." Anyone who is not "Black" by the standards of definition espoused by Black ghetto racists, almost all of whom are career criminals, are regarded as outsiders Black racists feel entitled to commit crimes against because they are "not one of us." Ghetto culture glorifies criminals, including Black racist criminals, and marginalizes outsiders, crime victims in general, and Whites in particular.

Black Racism In The Media

The mass media occasionally carry news stories that include video recordings of Blacks, often in gangs or smaller wolf-pack groups, attacking a lone White in public places such as restaurants. Black racists do this because they are of the opinion that the lone White individual wore unusual clothing, or were guilty of being White, or some other sort of everyday behavior that the Blacks in question saw as an excuse for violence. This is a ghetto overseer mentality.

Ghetto culture legitimizes random violence against Whites at the personal discretion of Black racist criminals and marginalizes their victims for bogus reasons such a White's clothing, speech or other aspects of their personal behavior. Black criminals often say words to the effect that White crime victims "had it coming" or that the attackers "didn't mean it" (a standard characterization of Black-on-White criminal behavior) or "that's the way Black people are, don't get in their way."

Blacks racist usually believe that they are "entitled" to commit crimes against Whites without fear of punishment. They are the products of a lower-class ghetto culture where violence is the norm and violent criminals are idolized. Ghetto culture hates and envies Whites, so ghetto culture say that anything goes where Whites are involved.

One common symptom of everyday Black racism is Black beggars asking White strangers on the street, to "loan" them money. Ghetto culture legitimizes lying to Whites and defrauding them of money. Such beggars should apply for loan from their parole officers. If they don't have one as yet, they will have one eventually.

Black-initiated violence against Whites for no real reason is not a topic that Black racists talk about. Their disregard for the interests of White crime victims reflect their Black racist overseer mentality. Violence is the norm when Blacks feel like doing it to Whites. However, White self-defense and the criminal prosecution of Black criminals are taboo subjects for Black racists.

White victims of Black racist crimes are quite aware that some Blacks routinely pretend not to see Black-On-White crimes that go on right in front of them. Blacks of the pro-criminal mentality never cooperate with the legal system to punish Blacks for crimes, and don't care about the White victims of such crimes, because they see no need to respect Whites in any way. Blacks who don't report crimes do so because they see criminal activities as the normal way of life in the ghetto where many Blacks believe they are entitled to commit crimes.

Many Blacks see no evil, hear no evil and speak no evil regarding Black-on-White crimes. This applies to theft and bullying in schools, fraudulent charges of racism on the job and street crime. Their viewpoint is that whatever happens to a White person that is perpetrated by a Black racist is something that they couldn't care less about. The only time that they care is when a Black criminal is caught, at which point they charge the White crime victim with being a racist.

Chapter Seven
The Psychology
Of Black Racism

Chapter Seven
The Psychology Of
Black Racism

Black Racism And Crime

Scratch a Black racist and you will usually find a career criminal not too far beneath the surface. Consider the example of a typical Black racist. No education worthy of the name in the sense of knowing anything worth knowing about history, literature, mathematics, physics, biology, law or any other subject. He may even have a high school diploma by virtue of having been promoted automatically by the sort of ghetto high schools that Black racists are likely to attend. He probably majored in gang activity, in the sense of having spent more time with street gang members during the course of a day than being physically present in high school.

During school and after school, gang members talk about, and practice, engaging in different sorts of crimes. After school lets out, gang members go out and engage in criminal activities with other gang members. They attacks members of other gangs, and attacks students and adults whom they think have money. They attack others because that is what gang members do. Actual and potential violence is always a possibility in the ghetto. Ghetto criminals cannot support themselves. They commit crimes to force others to support them against their will.

One thing gang members learn early in their criminal careers is how to use violence and threats to intimidate their crime victims into not filing criminal charges. The only way they can stay out of prison is to make sure that nobody gets a chance to put them into prison. Intimidating witnesses is an illegal that gang members are not likely to worry about. . Gang members kill, maim and torture people they dislike.

Black Racists Hate "Snitches"

One common theme in Black ghetto society is the near-universal deference given to the perpetrators of crimes against Whites, This is accompanied by a hatred of snitches, meaning crime victims and crime witnesses who choose to exercise their freedom of speech to inform parties who are more powerful than the perpetrators of a crime, such as the government, about the commission of crimes.

Two principles are at work. First is ghetto residents' identification with the aggressors, meaning imitative admiration for the perpetrators of criminal activities, particularly criminal activities directed against Whites by Blacks. This form of prejudiced idolization of criminals is accompanied by the marginalization of their victims. Many ghetto residents identify with career criminals, and some may very well go on to become imitative perpetrators of similar crimes in the future.

Second is the refusal on the part of Black ghetto criminals to see crime victims, particularly White crime victims, as having any rights of any kind that crime perpetrator must respect. Everything about ghetto culture and Black racism pushes them in that direction, and only the fear of punishment holds many of them back. Ghetto criminals hate and envy Whites and feel entitled to commit crimes against them because they hate and envy them.

Black racist criminals think that they are entitled to commit crimes against Whites because they were raised in a lower-class Black ghetto culture that encouraged them to think like that. They see potential crime victims the way that hungry wolf packs see stray rabbits, meaning as targets of opportunity. Ghetto criminals actually demand that others respect them for violating the rights of others, which is why you should not respect them in any way. This topsy-turvy inversion of the way normal people see the world is the result of ghetto criminals having internalized ghetto cultural values. The White middle class thus has no common ground with ghetto criminals.

Ghetto residents idolize and admire professional criminals because they set the tone for ghetto culture. John Locke noted that "Robberies, murders, rapes, are the sports of men set at liberty from punishment." The ghetto's social elite of career criminals set the standards for ghetto culture, which includes making crime victims into non-persons. In the world of ghetto culture, crime victims have no rights that the ghetto respects.

Ghetto criminals characterize witnesses, informants and crime victims as "snitches." They define crime victims in this derogatory manner in order to denigrate, delegitimize and thereby marginalize crime victims and witnesses in order to discourage legal retaliation by victims against the perpetrators of crimes. Criminals who get caught and sent to prison do not voluntarily pay restitution to their crime victims because that is contrary to ghetto culture. Criminals don't respect crime victims, so crime victims should never respect criminals. Ghetto criminals are never repentant because ghetto culture has institutionalized disrespect for crime victims.

Criminals who wind up in prison spend a great deal of time thinking about how they wound up there, and often dwell on those who filed criminal charges against them or testified against them. In the context of the ghetto, criminals consider themselves to be important. In prison, they are just perps with numbers. They thus hate people who helped punish them. When prisoners commit crimes against other inmates, the threat of retaliation against informant snitches is so great that informants often have to be put into a special part of a prison to protect them from violent retaliation.

The fact of the matter is that the perpetrators of crimes are the ones who are fully to blame for the crimes they commit and snitches should be accorded hero status. Blame the perps for their criminal activities, not their victims. People who make excuses for violent criminals because they identify with the aggressor should be considered to be potentially dangerous. Those who take the side of crime perpetrators cannot be trusted. Blacks who look down on snitches are either dangerous or potentially dangerous precisely because they have no regard for the welfare of crime victims.

If you are attacked by a Black felon who works on the loading dock at your company, do not expect the Black file clerk who says that she hates snitches to call the police or help you in any way. Black racists are not your friends, and Blacks who identify with Black racist criminal aggressors are also not your friends.

Black Groupthink Racism

When a group of people get together with others who think as they do, they often find themselves going along with the consensus opinion regarding almost every subject, no matter how stupid the consensus might be. This sort of thing often happens in companies that are on the wrong track, know that they are on the wrong track, but refuse to acknowledge, let along take action on, the unspoken feeling that something is wrong. This is groupthink. Nobody is willing to speak up because the gold standard for group behavior is to not make waves.

After the passage of time in the groupthink state, people simply stop thinking for themselves and just follow precedents established under the influence of the group consensus. Such people repress the individual parts of their personalities, block their ability to think as individuals, and eventually become nearly-interchangeable conformists,

This is what happens in ghetto street gangs. The ghetto consensus is that education is bad because it is "White." Gang members drop out of school, learn how to be criminals in the ghetto's unofficial college of crime and graduate into the world of street crime. Whites are their preferred targets of opportunity, though Asians, Blacks who act "White" and Africans of foreign birth also suit them just fine as potential crime victims. The examples of Asians and foreign-born Blacks who live in ghettos, go to school, start businesses and go on to move out of the ghetto show that Black criminality is simply the result of Black willingness to go along with the ghetto street gang behavioral consensus.

Blacks like to blame Whites for ghetto crime, but Whites are nowhere to be found in the ghetto. Whites do not come into the ghetto to teach Blacks how to commit crimes. Whites do not come into the ghetto to force Blacks to drop out of school. Whites do not come into the ghetto to teach Blacks how to commit crimes. Whites do not come into the ghetto to invite violent Black racists to come to White neighborhoods to commit crimes against. Blacks are fully responsible for all of these things, but pretend that someone else is the cause because criminals never accept blame for their actions.

Roving wolf packs of Black criminals cruising through White neighborhoods in search of crime victims constitute one example of Black-on-White criminal racism in action. Violence focused on Whites as a group is racism. Threats focused on Whites as a group as a group is racism. Reverse discrimination in the workplace focused on White as a group is racism. Street crime focused on Whites as a group is racism. Any thoughts, words or actions that categorize Whites as potential victims of subordination or victimization by Blacks, particularly Black criminals, constitutes racism on the part of Blacks, and this is most common among Black with a xenophobic criminal mentality, and ghetto gang members are the worst offenders.

Chapter Eight
Other Forms Of Black Racism

Chapter Eight
Other Forms Of Black Racism

Black Racists Hate Blacks Who Act White

Black racism is often found as a byproduct of Black ghetto criminal gang membership. Gang members define outsiders, including Blacks who are not gang members, as fair game for gang members. Whites are neither gang members nor Black, so they are seen by ethnocentric Black racist gang members as complete outsiders, meaning undifferentiated, interchangeable potential targets for gang crimes.

Talking Black means speaking in an ungrammatical, uneducated, heavily-accented English dialect that few Whites, including employers, can comprehend without mental strain of a magnitude that few employers will care to make.

Talking Black is a linguistic form of Black ethnocentric solidarity takes the form of xenophobic rejection of formal education because they define it as "White," meaning the speech patterns of the formally educated with prospects for participation in the mainstream job market.

"Talking White" means the speech of a Black male or female who speaks in grammatical English, or with an accent reminiscent of Whites. Such Blacks are often derided and harassed by Black racists as "race traitors" for the offense of speaking in a manner disapproved of by local Black high-school dropouts on the fast track for permanent unemployment or prison.

The Black racists' viewpoint is that talking even a little bit White means "not being Black enough" to suit the opinions of Black racists. Ethnocentric Blacks demand conformity of all Blacks, even if conformity makes them unemployable.

Those who fail to learn how to talk "White," meaning talk in a way that makes them readily comprehensible and employable, are headed for trouble. The only prospects on their economic horizons will be the underground criminal economy and spending time in the penitentiary. The ethnocentric linguistic expectations that Black hard-core unemployables demand of other Blacks preclude them from participating in the mainstream job market.

Street talk is for ghetto types who don't want to fit into the "White" job market. Be aware that the derogatory street slang terms used to characterize Whites are inherently racist in and of themselves, and constitute evidence of a lack of respect for Whites and White culture.

Differences Matter

Black racists crack down hard on Blacks they perceive to be "acting White" or "talking White." This includes foreign-born Blacks from Africa and the Caribbean. Black racists attack Asians and foreign-born Blacks as well as Whites, which shows that the "legacy of slavery" has nothing to do with their criminal behavior. Asians and foreign-born Blacks are two groups that had nothing to do with slavery. Black racists are simply violent, opportunistic criminals who will attack any target within sight to steal money or attempt to control the property and actions of other people through threats and violence, and they see Asians and foreign-born Blacks as targets of opportunity.

Contemporary Asians came to this country long after slavery ended, but Black racist criminals attack them just as they attack Whites because they stay in school, save their money, stay out of prison and move up in the world in economic terms. American Black criminals also attack Black immigrants from the Caribbean and Africa. Many foreign-born Blacks come to the United States not even knowing English, but stay in school, start up small businesses in the ghettos and move on to bigger and better things outside the ghettos.

Black racist criminals attack Asians and foreign-born Blacks who come to America because it is in the nature of criminals to victimize anybody they can find. Career criminals believe that they are entitled to commit crimes against anybody they choose according to the standards of the ghetto culture that trains and encourages them to become career criminals. Whites owe them nothing.

Ghetto culture leads them to believe that they are entitled to avoid being punished for crimes. They thus attempt blame their criminal activities on anybody other than themselves, which is why they bring up the legacy of slavery so often while never bringing up the examples of foreign-born Blacks and Asians. They envy those who have done better than they have, meaning anybody who stayed in school and works for a living, which includes Whites, Asians, foreign-born blacks and Blacks who talk "White."

Asians and foreign-born Blacks come to the United States, get jobs, avoid lives of crime, start small businesses which employ their family members, require their children to stay in school and study every night, go to college, and move up economically. Eventually they move out of the ghetto and leave ghetto criminals behind in the dust.

Asians and foreign-born Blacks don't waste their lives whining that Whites "never gave them a chance," they just get on with their lives. Ghetto criminals had the same chances as the Asians, foreign-born Blacks and Whites, but decided to drop out of school and join street gangs, so they must pay the price for refusing to study and work for a living. Whites, Asians and foreign-born blacks do not owe ghetto criminals a living. Ghetto criminals don't like to see or hear about people moving up in the world because their example makes ghetto criminals look like pathetic losers in the game of life, so they make them into crime victims.

Black racists decide to become dropouts at an early age and wind up spending the rest of their lives paying for their adolescent stupidity. They deliberately chose to not become educated, they deliberately chose to not put in a full day's work for a full day's pay, they deliberately chose to not plan for the future, they deliberately chose to not learn how to start up a business, they deliberately chose to not to do anything of any kind that will move them out of the bottom of the heap, so no other results are possible. Inaction has consequences.

They become criminals by default because they deliberately chose to not become anything else. They are to blame for the choices they made. Whites owe them nothing, Asians owe them nothing and foreign-born Blacks owe them nothing.

Chapter Nine
Legal Options

Chapter Nine
Legal Options

Black Racism In The Workplace

One sure sign that Black racists have a friend in the human resources, or personnel, department is that when a company chooses to employ a number of Black felons, those felons work together under the supervision of a Black criminal who has several lesser convictions but no felony convictions as yet. When Whites are forced into workplace groups of this nature, all sorts of things always seem to go wrong for the Whites.

Felons are experienced bullies. Black felons see Whites as their natural targets because felons think that they are entitled to commit crimes whenever they feel like doing so. That is what they learned growing up in the ghettos and while in prison. They are much less cognizant that Whites are entitled to press criminal charges against them without warning.

One sign that a company gives employment preference to Black felons is that few Black employees can be seen wearing name badges. They do this because they do not want anyone to know their names, particularly the sort of coworkers who like to read about crimes in the news. Black felons always seem to sit together in the cafeteria, and many of them have visible knife scars, gang tattoos and needle marks.

One sign that you are working with a Black criminal occurs when new employees attempt to get you under their control as soon as they enter the workplace, which is actually a thinly-disguised attempt to dominate any and all Whites with whom they have contact. A new recruit at a food service might attempt to direct and control experienced employees involved in food preparation despite knowing nothing about how to do the work and insist that he is right despite being wrong in every way.

Their model for social interactions is street gangs where they engage in what Whites would characterize as being disruptively pushy behavior. Ghetto culture legitimizes pushing Whites around at will, including Whites that know how to do the job better than they can, so nothing better can be expected of them.

It is distressingly common in workplaces for groups of Black racist felons to gang up on one White because that White is White. Black racists will often attempt to attack isolated Whites who are forced to work with Blacks and have them terminated on the basis of fraudulent charges of racism. They do this to Whites because Black racists hate and envy Whites as a race. This makes them racists. They refuse to accept Whites being in their previously all-Black work environments. The only way that they can pretend to be important is to victimize Whites. Ghetto culture legitimizes this as an acceptable form of on-the-job recreation. You can be absolutely sure that every Black felon who has contact with any White person will call him a racist.

Black felons often gravitate towards unskilled manual labor jobs because they are completely unqualified for anything else due to having dropped out of high school. It is standard operating procedure for Black racist felons to work together as a gang to work over victims in the workplace and on the street. Black racist felons think that "anything goes" if they feel like doing it to Whites.

Middle-class Blacks who do not live in ghettos are capable of racism. It all depends on what they say, think and do with respect to Whites as individuals or as a group. If they have internalized and accepted the beliefs of ghetto criminals which legitimize discrimination against Whites and marginalize Whites as a group, they are Black racists.

A middle-class Black racist who works in a corporate human resources department might have opportunities to discriminate against Whites in matters of hiring, firing, workplace discrimination and conflict resolution. If he chooses to actually engage in such activities, he is a Black racist.

When Blacks acquire hierarchical power within organizations such as corporations because they hold certain jobs, they may have opportunities to engage in racist and discriminatory activities. Prejudice on the part of Blacks combined with power over Whites equals Black racism when such Blacks take actions that discriminate against Whites or take actions that produce anti-White results, such as refusing to consider job applications from Whites. Some Blacks engage in racism and racial discrimination while others do not.

If the White victim complains to somebody in the company's personnel department, nobody in the personnel department that hired those felons seems to care about what sort of experiences that White victim had. Nobody in the personnel department seems to be interested in White crime victims of Black racists, and everybody in personnel seems to be falling all over themselves to cater to the Black racist felons.

Personnel department directors are not your friends. Staff members of personnel departments smile while engaging in reverse discrimination against Whites. They are the ones who hired the sort of Black racist felons who harass Whites on the job. You are not on their list of priorities because they do not consider you to be a priority, and will be disinclined to take any action on your behalf when the Black racist felons they hired create problems for you on the job. Personnel departments see their first responsibility as being to themselves and their relatives, their second responsibility as being to their race, and their third responsibility as being to their companies.

You will find that corporate personnel departments which discriminate against Whites also often engage in a second form of routine anti-White racism. They routinely go out of their way to hire illegal aliens to replace US citizens in their workplace and go on to lie about it despite overwhelming evidence in the form of employees who do not read, write or speak English.

Anti-White racism is thus a two-headed monster. Racists in personnel departments thus discriminate against White citizens in two ways. Both methods of discrimination are illegal but are rarely punished. They always claim to have no knowledge whatsoever of what they did. Blame the perpetrators, not the victims.

Taking Action In The Workplace

There are several ways that Whites can have Black racist criminals who attack, harass, threaten or bother them in other ways terminated from employment.

The best option is to find out their names and obtain their criminal convictions, including felonies. If they do not wear identification badges with their names, then watch them when they punch out at the time clock. If they work in an office, look at the name plates on their desks or doors. Once you have their names, look up the criminal records of the Black criminals with whom you work either at the local courthouse or an online national database.

Criminal records are public records that anybody can obtain copy, mail out, talk about and publicize. Criminal records are not "private." Anybody who tells you that criminal records are private is a liar and quite likely to be a criminal or someone who identifies with them. Be sure to also look at traffic court records, many Black racists have warrants out for their arrest for drunk driving and related offenses. Civil court records, such court records about illegal anti-White employment discrimination perpetrated by companies, are also public records.

The next step is to send out anonymous letters to the company's human resources vice present, company president, board of directors or all of the above parties at corporate headquarters with the names, felony conviction case numbers, workplace locations and other identifying information. Tell them in your letters that a felon, or several felons, they hired may very possibly have lied on their job application about being a felon. This is known as employment fraud. Do not send your letters to the local personnel department that hired them, they will simply throw them out.

Mailing a notice about possible employment fraud by one or more felons works best in cases of large national companies such as national restaurant chains and retail chains. Never send criminal conviction information to local personnel managers. They created the problem, so they should deal with the ultimate consequences of their actions. Be aware that they might decide to terminate you on bogus charges if they find out that you were responsible for exposing the felons they hired, so do everything anonymously.

Another alternative is to contact the company's insurance company, which may be interested in issues personnel departments do not tell White employees about, such as a series of seemingly inexplicable thefts from the company's warehouse or food service. When companies replace Black ghetto felons with Blacks from the suburbs, these problems seem to fade away quite rapidly.

Black felons believe that they are entitled to lie whenever they feel like it, including on job applications, because it is in their nature to victimize people and groups of people such as companies. The truth of the matter is that they are not entitled to commit employment fraud, and companies will not retain people who commit employment fraud once they find out about it.

Employers are entitled to terminate Black felons who commit employment fraud, and almost all companies will automatically terminate people who engage in employment fraud by lying on job applications, particularly about having criminal records. The way that many such felons get hired is to have a Black in the human resources department who identifies with felon aggressors either skip over the pre-employment criminal record check or simply engage in a racial preference when hiring Black dropout felons in preference to White educated non-criminals.

Civil court legal actions regarding matters such as employment and promotion discrimination should begin with your personal lawyer, not the personnel department that created the problem. If you attempt to file a lawsuit without a lawyer, you can expect to learn the hard way that he who acts as his own lawyer has a fool for a client. Never tell anyone you work with that you are planning a lawsuit or you may find yourself terminated on bogus charges in short order. If a company terminates you after you file a lawsuit against them, they are likely to experience some legal problems.

Black Racism In The Workplace

Most Black criminals are also racists, and should always be considered potentially dangerous in the physical sense of the word. People who make excuses for them are themselves potentially dangerous.

Black racist felons don't want their potential victims, such as women they work with, to know how dangerous they actually have shown themselves to be in the past. One sign that you are dealing with a potentially dangerous Black racist is that they say they will "hurt" someone for talking about their criminal records. Criminal records are public records. Anyone can get copies of them and do whatever they want with them. They can even put them in newspapers or on television. People who say that they do not want anybody to know about them are potentially dangerous.

Collect the names of any Black racists you are forced to work with. Look up their felony records and other criminal records in online national databases or at the local courthouse and make your plans based on what you discover. You are free to contact the police if you discover any cause for concern, such as an outstanding warrant for somebody's arrest.

If you work with a Black criminal who engages in verbal outbursts, threats, attempts to control Whites or similar behavior, they may either be facing trial for one or more crimes or have an outstanding warrant for their arrest. People who feel that they have nothing to lose often engage in such behavior. If they are on trial in a local court, a little bit of research will soon show you that their absences from work coincide with the days that they have been summoned to court. Threats are crimes, so mention them to the police if you are threatened. Criminal trials are public trials, and you are free to take a day off from work and drop in on their trials.

Do not allow anyone you have a bad feeling about, or whom you have determined to be a criminal, into your car, because they might plant evidence there or attack you. Do not accept a ride from them, because they may attack you or their car may be a stolen car. Do not respond to any attempts at interrogation or cross-examination.

Do not allow Black felons to touch you for any reason. Do not allow Black felons to whisper in your ear. Never comply with any demand made by a Black racist that they be allowed to speak with you in private, because such a demand is always a prelude to premeditated physical violence conducted out of the public eye, possibly as part of group. Career criminals cannot be trusted, so don't trust them.

Whites should be aware that nothing a felon says has any validity or meaning whatsoever in any court of law or with the police. That means that if a felon threatens you, attacks you, or both, and threatens you with malicious prosecution, they are both lying and should be regarded as verifiably dangerous, experienced criminals. Felons cannot have anyone arrested or prosecuted because a felon's word is legally invalid in both criminal and civil courts.

Telling you that they will take legal action against you for talking about a crime, or charging them with a crime, they committed against you is itself another category of crime that should add to their sentence.

If you see a need to contact the police about a threat or an attack in your workplace, do not tell the human resources department anything unless your personal lawyer says that it is in your personal best interest. It may turn out that the felon you filed a complaint against is a relative or a member of their church of the Black person in personnel who hired them. Do not warn or alert anybody in the company about your contacts with the police. If you do so, it will operate to your disadvantage, and you can be sure that the human resources department will tell the offending party everything that they learn from you.

It is important to allow the police to process the Black racist felons without any regard whatsoever for the impact on the company, other company employees and the company's personnel department. Whoever originally hired the Black racist felons does not want you to do anything that might endanger their job, such as sue someone responsible for hiring the felons, though they do not care in the slightest about the impact of felons they hired on you or other White victims. Let them pay the price, it will be a positive learning experience for the guilty parties. You owe nothing to people who endanger you.

Another concern regarding the personnel department staff members with whom you interact is that a visit by the police to either question or arrest an employee will find its way to the desk of the company's top management and that will both reflect poorly on the personnel department staff members who hired Black racist felons and may leave them open to the possibility of termination from their own jobs. They brought it on themselves, so they can deal with it themselves.

Assume that anything that personnel department staff members might say to you constitutes an attempt to intimidate you into not pressing charges, a matter which you are free to bring up with the police. Failing to press charges in the case of a threat or an attack is likely to put you back in daily contact with the person(s) you sought to file charges against or leave you open to a variety of legal problems. Consult your personal lawyer before you say anything to the personnel department.

If you contact the police after you have a problem with a Black criminal on the job, the personnel department may contact you and demand that you meet with them as a condition of continuing employment. You may have no choice but to go into their office. You need not do anything once you get there. Never sign anything they ask you to sign. If they say that signing something is just a "formality," tell them that having your lawyer look it over is just a "formality" as well.

Do not make a statement or describe the events that led to you contacting the police. They are quite likely to record what you say without your knowledge or consent, and go on use whatever you say to terminate you on bogus charges. Personnel departments are staffed with professional liars, so think of them and treat them as professional liars.

When you are in the personnel department office, you are free to keep repeating that you do not consent to be recorded and that you will definitely report your conversation with personnel to the police, district attorney and your own lawyer. You can also demand that your own lawyer be present.

Again, the personnel department staff members are not your friends. They do not work for you and you would not want anybody who hired Black racist felons and put them into contact with you as your friend. Be aware that company personnel files can be subpoenaed for use in court. If a company deliberately puts you into contact on the job with known criminals, you may be able to sue them them for damages.

Retain a lawyer as necessary, and use the law to make your workplace a Black racism-free zone.

Chapter Ten
Black-On-White Crime Statistics

Chapter Ten
Black-On-White
Crime Statistics

U.S. Population Statistics

Total Population: 307,007,000 (100.0%)
White Population: 244,298,000 (79.5%)
Black Population: 39,641,000 (12.9%

U.S. Census Bureau *2011 Statistical Abstract Of The United States* "Table 19. Resident Population By Race, Hispanic Origin, And State: 2009" http://www.census.gov/compendia/statab/

Homicide Statistics

56% of all homicides were committed by Blacks.
16.4 % of all White homicides were committed by Blacks.
6.9% of all Black homicides were committed by Whites.

U.S. Department Of Justice,
Office Of Justice Programs
Bureau Of Justice Statistics
Homicide Trends In The U.S
James Alan Fox And Marianne W. Zawitz,
http://bjs.ojp.usdoj.gov/content/pub/pdf/htius.pdf

Rape Statistics

50.4% of all rapes were committed by Blacks.
33% of all rapes/sexual assaults of Whites were committed by Blacks.
0% of all rapes of Blacks were committed by Whites.

U.S. Department of Justice,
Office of Justice Programs
Bureau of Justice Statistics
Criminal Victimization in the United States, 2005, Statistical Tables
"Table 42. Personal Crimes Of Violence, 2005:
Percent Distribution Of Single-Offender Victimizations,
Based On Race Of Victims, By Type Of Crime And Perceived Race Of Offender." http://bjs.ojp.usdoj.gov/content/pub/pdf/cvus05.pdf

Robbery Statistics

38.6% of all robberies were committed by Blacks.
27.8% of all robberies of Whites were committed by Blacks.
4.9% of all robberies of Blacks were committed by Whites.

U.S. Department of Justice,
Office of Justice Programs
Bureau of Justice Statistics
Criminal Victimization in the United States, 2005, Statistical Tables
"Table 42. Personal Crimes Of Violence, 2005:
Percent Distribution Of Single-Offender Victimizations,
Based On Race Of Victims, By Type Of Crime And Perceived Race Of Offender." http://bjs.ojp.usdoj.gov/content/pub/pdf/cvus05.pdf

Court Cases And Other References

Court Cases And Other References

Court Cases

U. S. Supreme Court
Near v. Minnesota, 283 U.S. 697 (1931).

U. S. Supreme Court
Regents of the University of California v. Bakke, 438 U.S. 265 (1978).

U. S. Supreme Court
Ricci v. DeStefano, 07-1428 (2009).

John Peter Zenger
The Trial Of John Peter Zenger (1735).

Government Documents

U.S. Census Bureau
2011 Statistical Abstract Of The United States
"Table 19. Resident Population By Race, Hispanic Origin, And State: 2009"
http://www.census.gov/compendia/statab

U.S. Department of Justice,
Office of Justice Programs,
Bureau of Justice Statistics
Criminal Victimization in the United States, 2005, Statistical Tables
"Table 42. Personal Crimes Of Violence, 2005: Percent Distribution Of Single-Offender Victimizations, Based On Race Of Victims, By Type Of Crime And Perceived Race Of Offender."
http://bjs.ojp.usdoj.gov/content/pub/pdf/cvus05.pdf

U.S. Department of Justice,
Office of Justice Programs,
Bureau of Justice Statistics
Homicide Trends in the U.S
James Alan Fox and Marianne W. Zawitz,
http://bjs.ojp.usdoj.gov/content/pub/pdf/htius.pdf

U.S. Department of Justice,
Office of Justice Programs,
National Institute of Justice
The Code Of The Street And African-American Adolescent Violence Research In Brief. February 2009.
http://www.ojp.usdoj.gov/nij

Other References

William Blackstone
Blackstone's Commentaries, 1899.

Stanley M. Elkins
Slavery: A Problem In American Institutional And Intellectual Life, The University of Chicago Press, 1959.

Anna Freud
The Ego And The Mechanisms Of Defence
International Universities Press, 1946.

John Locke
Essay Concerning Human Understanding, 1689.

Niccolo Machiavelli
The Historical, Political, and Diplomatic Writings of Niccolo Machiavelli, Discourses 1882.

Charles Mackay
Life And Liberty In America: Or, Sketches Of A Tour In The United States And Canada In 1857-8, Harper And Brothers, 1859.

John Stuart Mill
Early Essays: Bentham 1897.

Norman Podhoretz
"My Negro Problem – And Ours"
Commentary February, 1963, pages 93-101.

Kenneth M. Stampp
The Peculiar Institution: Slavery in the Ante-Bellum South, Alfred A. Knopf, 1956.
Harriet Beecher Stowe
Uncle Tom's Cabin, 1852.

William Graham Sumner
Folkways: A Study Of The Sociological Importance Of Usages, Manners, Customs, Mores, And Morals, 1906.

Carter G. Woodson
Free Negro Owners Of Slaves In The United States In 1830, Together With Absentee Ownership Of Slaves In The United States In 1830, 1924.

Made in the USA
Middletown, DE
17 July 2016